NATIONAL GEOGRAPHIC

Wood

Kate McGough

What things are made of wood?

My blocks are made of wood.

My chair is made of wood.
My table is made of wood.

My puzzle is made of wood.

Where does wood come from?

Wood comes from trees.

We use the wood from trees to make things.